GLORIA
STEINEM
CHAMPION OF WOMEN'S RIGHTS

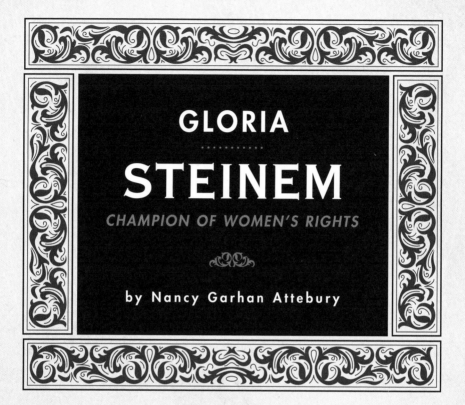

GLORIA
STEINEM

CHAMPION OF WOMEN'S RIGHTS

by Nancy Garhan Attebury

Content Adviser: Joyce Henricks, Ph.D.,
Departments of Philosophy and Religion and
Women's Studies, Central Michigan University

Reading Adviser: Rosemary G. Palmer, Ph.D.,
Department of Literacy, College of Education,
Boise State University

COMPASS POINT BOOKS ✦ MINNEAPOLIS, MINNESOTA

Compass Point Books
3109 West 50th Street, #115
Minneapolis, MN 55410

Visit Compass Point Books on the Internet at *www.compasspointbooks.com*
or e-mail your request to *custserv@compasspointbooks.com*

Editor: Jennifer VanVoorst
Page Production: Noumenon Creative
Photo Researcher: Marcie C. Spence
Cartographer: XNR Productions, Inc.
Library Consultant: Kathleen Baxter

Art Director: Jaime Martens
Creative Director: Keith Griffin
Editorial Director: Carol Jones
Managing Editor: Catherine Neitge

*I wish to dedicate this book to my mother, Roseletta Garhan, my daughter,
Ramirose Attebury Wendt, my friend Penny Gabrielson, and my late friends
LeAnn Hoffman and Janeen Tuning. They are all strong women who taught
me to soar. A special thank you to Gloria Steinem, who graciously granted
me interviews. NGA*

Library of Congress Cataloging-in-Publication Data
Attebury, Nancy Garhan
  Gloria Steinem: Champion of Women's Rights / by Nancy
Garhan Attebury.
      p. cm. — (Signature lives)
  Includes bibliographical references and index.
  ISBN 0-7565-1587-4 (hardcover)
  1. 2. Feminists—United States—Biography—Juvenile literature. 3.
Feminism—United States—Juvenile literature. I. Title. II. Series.
  HQ1413.S675A77 2006
  305.42'092—dc22   2005025208

Signature Lives

MODERN AMERICA

Starting in the late 19th century, advancements in all areas of human activity transformed an old world into a new and modern place. Inventions prompted rapid shifts in lifestyle, and scientific discoveries began to alter the way humanity viewed itself. Beginning with World War I, warfare took place on a global scale, and ideas such as nationalism and communism showed that countries were taking a larger view of their place in the world. The combination of all these changes continues to produce what we know as the modern world.

Gloria Steinem

Table of Contents

1 A BUNNY'S TALE

❧❧❧

Gloria Steinem pulled on her thin black tights, scratchy orange costume with the fluffy bunny tail, matching shoes, and bunny ears. Then she smoothed the costume and began her work shift. She had not expected her job serving drinks and checking coats as a Playboy bunny to be so physically unpleasant, but the uncomfortable costume and endless hours on her feet made her miserable. She had wrapped her ribs in gauze to ease the pain of the tight suit. She glanced at her swollen feet. Her tight shoes with three-inch heels made her feet swell. She would need to borrow bigger ones to finish her shift.

In 1963, many young women worked at the Playboy Club because they needed the money, but Steinem already had a job. She worked for a magazine

Gloria Steinem worked undercover as a Playboy bunny in order to write a story exposing job conditions and employee treatment.

In the late 1800s, investigative reporter Nellie Bly went undercover to get facts for newspaper articles. She pretended to be mentally ill in order to investigate a mental institution from the inside. She wrote about the horrible conditions and the way people there were treated. Her real name was Elizabeth Cochrane, but she used the pen name Nellie Bly because newspaper work at the time was not considered a respectable job for women. Her articles prompted change and brought new respect to women in journalism.

called *Show*. She was working undercover as a Playboy bunny to gather information so that she could write a story about the job.

Steinem took on her undercover role with a sense of adventure. Before she went to her job interview, she created a fake identity using old family names. On her application, she called herself Marie Catherine Ochs, after her maternal grandmother. She also listed her age as younger than her 29 years.

To Steinem's surprise, she was hired and began working at New York City's Playboy Club. She and the other young women checked patrons' coats and waited tables, but Steinem had additional work to do: She paid close attention to the working conditions and morale of the other women. She wondered if they felt safe and found their jobs rewarding. She wondered if their salaries were as promised and if they felt good about themselves.

Steinem felt awful. She pulled on her tight orange costume or her skimpy blue one nightly for nearly

Gloria Steinem picketed for the cause of women's rights.

three weeks. Her face was covered with thick makeup and fake eyelashes. During that time, she lost weight and was extremely tired.

Steinem had been promised $200 to $300 a week in pay, but when she quit after three weeks, she only received $35.90. Her employers had misrepresented the rate of pay. But she did get what she wanted. The job gave her the information she needed to write an article called "I Was a Playboy Bunny." In the article, Steinem wrote about issues the women faced, including low wages, long hours, abusive customers, and physically uncomfortable working conditions. The experience gave her new insight into how women were viewed and treated by men and helped lay the groundwork for her growing feminist beliefs.

The article brought Steinem instant fame, but not the type she wanted. Her life's dream was to be a good journalist. But the common view at the time said a woman's name should be in the newspaper only three times in her life: when she was born, when she was married, and when she died. That idea hindered Steinem. Furthermore, her appearance made it hard for the public to take her seriously as a writer. She longed to write about serious and important topics, but the public did not believe that a beautiful woman could write intelligently about politics and social issues.

Despite the many roadblocks, Gloria Steinem challenged this misguided belief and triumphed.

Feminism is the belief that women are entitled to the same rights that men enjoy. Feminists believe that men and women should receive equal pay for equal work and have the same chance to fill a job opening. Feminists challenge traditional beliefs that limit women's roles. They argue that women can work on construction crews or become astronauts, and men can help with housework and care for children.

In the 1960s, a new wave of feminism was spreading across the United States, and Steinem became a leader of the growing movement. Through her writings, speeches, and programs, she has challenged many of society's injustices and brought attention to the plight of those who live on society's fringes. Over the course of her long and groundbreaking career, she has been a champion of the civil rights movement, fighting for equality for African-Americans. She has worked as an advocate for low-paid farmworkers. But more

Steinem signed autographs for supporters during a 1975 protest rally.

Steinem spoke out on behalf of a woman seeking asylum in the United States.

than anything, she is known for her outspoken and unflagging fight for the rights of women.

Steinem has accomplished much and continues

to do more to better the way of life for others. *Ms.*, the magazine she helped found, continues to spread an important feminist message, and organizations she helped create, such as the National Women's Political Caucus and the Women's Action Alliance, still work to further the cause of women. As a result of her tireless efforts, Steinem has become one of the United States' most well-known political activists and one of the leading feminists of the 20th century. For many, it is her face and her words that represent the modern women's movement. Along with her fellow feminists, Steinem's efforts on behalf of women everywhere have moved society closer to equality—a world in which a girl can grow up to become anything she wants to be. ❧

In 1963, a Russian woman was the first female in space. In 1978, six U.S. women were picked to train for space. In 1983, Sally Ride, a member of this group, became the first U.S. woman in space. Now, many women are astronauts. Women have worked as pilots, space walkers, and launch commanders.

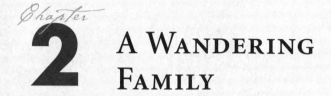

2 A WANDERING FAMILY

When Gloria Marie Steinem was born on March 25, 1934, she brought hope to a family that was suffering. Gloria's mother, Ruth, had experienced a nervous breakdown four years earlier, after giving birth to a stillborn son. The medicine she was prescribed helped calm her down, but when she took it, she slept for hours. She spent many months in a sanitarium before returning to her family in Clarklake, Michigan.

Like most families in the United States at the time, the Steinem family was suffering financially as well. The stock market had crashed in 1929, plunging the country into the Great Depression. Banks closed, and people were poor and hungry. Many lost everything they had. Gloria's father, Leo, held onto most of his properties, but the family still struggled.

As a young girl, Gloria Steinem had dreams of fame and fortune as a musician or dancer.

The Great Depression was a worldwide economic slump during the 1930s. It ranked as the worst and longest period of high unemployment and low business activity in the 20th century. Banks, factories, and shops closed, and farms halted production. Millions of people were left jobless and penniless. Many people had to depend on the government or charity to provide them with food.

Gloria's birth in 1934 brought a sense of hope to the Steinem family. For 9-year-old Susanne Steinem, a baby sister was a dream come true. Susanne was even allowed to name the new baby. She chose the name Gloria, after a favorite doll. Gloria's middle name, Marie, came from the girls' grandmother.

Gloria's parents and older sister had lived in Toledo, Ohio, until 1930. That year, they moved to Clarklake, Michigan, where the Steinems owned a resort called Ocean Beach Pier. Times were tight, and living at the resort was cheaper than in Ohio. The family earned money from guests who paid to stay at the resort. But Leo was never quite able to keep the family afloat. He often bought land without telling Ruth, and he spent more money on his projects than he made. Gloria put on a convincing act to help him when she was about 3 or 4. Every time a bill collector came to the door, she opened the door and said that her daddy was gone. Wide-eyed and innocent, she kept the collectors away.

In the summer, Leo hired big bands to play at the resort and entertain guests. He dreamed of bright

Clarklake was a popular vacation destination.

lights, show business, and wealth. Though he never became wealthy or famous, he chased money and fame all his life. Gloria dreamed of show business just like Leo. Ruby Brown, a young woman who worked at the resort's dance hall, taught Gloria to tap dance. Once Gloria learned the basic steps, she couldn't stop dancing. Sometimes she even started to dance on the street corner. Leo and Gloria felt her talent might lead to fame and fortune one day.

As a little girl, Gloria was free to roam around the family's resort. She played on the beach, often spending entire days in her bathing suit. Ruth made Gloria wear a red swimsuit so that she could easily see where Gloria was. Gloria grew to hate that suit so much that when she was 11, she bought herself a black swimsuit and has never worn a red one since.

Gloria recalled summers at Ocean Beach Pier:

> *[They were] a great time of running wild, catching turtles and minnows and setting them free again, looking for coins that customers at my parents' dance hall dropped in the lake, wearing a bathing suit all day long and sleeping in a little office behind the dance hall to the sounds of Gene Krupa or Wayne King or the Andrews Sisters.*

Though there was a nine-year age difference, Gloria and her sister had a close relationship. Gloria remembered, "I drove Susanne crazy by wanting to go everywhere she went in the summers!" She tagged along with her sister to the roller-skating rink at the other end of the lake and invited herself to the movies with Susanne and her girlfriends.

Summers at Ocean Beach Pier were a lovely time for Gloria, but by October or November, it was too cold to live at the resort. The buildings lacked heat because they were built for summer use. In the winter, Gloria was pulled out of school, and the family packed into a cramped house trailer, heading for the warmer climates of Florida or California. Ruth had

Ruth, Leo, Susanne, and Gloria Steinem posed for a family portrait shortly before Susanne left for college.

a teaching certificate, and she tutored Susanne and Gloria on the road. Leo worked as an antiques dealer while they traveled, and his sales paid family living expenses—though just barely. Money was always short, and the family's financial insecurity did not help Ruth's already unstable mental health.

Ruth was not well, but Susanne and Gloria knew

Gloria and her family spent winters traveling around the country in a house trailer.

how much she loved them. Gloria recalled, "Over and over again, in every way she knew how, she told us that we didn't need to earn her love. We were loved and valued (and therefore we were lovable and valuable) exactly as we were."

Gloria and her father had an especially close relationship. When Gloria was about 9, Leo took her to a store in nearby Jackson, Michigan. He stayed in the car and instructed her to go in and buy her own clothes. He always had high expectations of his daughter and respected her as an independent and capable person, even at a young age. In her 1990 essay, "The Unopposite Sex," Steinem recalled her father:

> *He treated me like a friend, asked my advice, enjoyed my company, and thus let me know that I was loved. Even in the hardest times, of which there were many, I knew with a child's unerring sense of fairness that he was treating me as well as he treated himself. … Against all he had been taught a man's life should be, against all convention for raising children and especially little girls, he loved and honored me as a unique person. And that let me know that he and I—and men and women—are not opposites after all.*

Through his example, Leo Steinem helped shape the attitudes of his daugher, and she in turn helped shape those of the world. 🙠

3 TOUGH TIMES IN TOLEDO

❧❦❧

In the early 1940s, declining tourism led to the failure of Ocean Beach Pier, and the Steinems closed their resort. The closure put a lot of stress on the family, and in 1944, when Gloria was 10 years old, Ruth and Leo separated. The split shattered Gloria's world. She and her mother moved to Amherst, Massachusetts, to be near Susanne, who was a student at Smith College.

Gloria, now in fifth grade, began to attend school regularly for the first time. She was sharp-minded and had been able to read by age 4, but she had spent most of her time reading fiction. She found she had a lot to learn about subjects like math and science. But she enjoyed playing ball and making friends at school, and she felt that she fit in. Ruth's mental condition had become more stable. For once, Gloria's childhood

Gloria's life took a turn for the better when she moved to Washington, D.C., for her senior year of high school.

> Gloria stayed in touch with her father after her parents divorced. Leo moved to California, although he spent a great deal of time on the road selling antiques. Gloria and he exchanged letters and saw each other once or twice a year.

appeared normal.

At the end of the school year, however, Ruth and Gloria moved to Scarsdale, New York, to be closer to Susanne, who had taken a summer job in New York City. Ruth's depression returned, and Gloria's "normal" life disappeared. At the end of the summer, they moved again—this time to East Toledo, Ohio, where they lived in a one-room basement apartment. The cramped apartment was tucked behind the building's furnace. Ruth and Gloria slept in a set of bunk beds because two twin beds could not fit on the floor side by side. During this time, Ruth and Leo officially divorced. The divorce—and the living conditions—were tough on Gloria, and she often imagined a different life for herself. She later wrote:

> *Though I loved my parents and knew I wasn't adopted, I used to fantasize endlessly that my real parents would come get me and take me to a neat house with a room of my own, and a horse in a field next door.*

Gloria was about 12 years old before she attended a full year of school. She attended sixth

grade at Toledo's Monroe Elementary School. She made friends with a girl in her apartment house and enjoyed the social opportunities school provided. But when that school year ended, Ruth and Gloria packed up for yet another move.

This move took them to a large rambling house on Woodville Road that had been the home of Ruth's parents. The run-down house now held three apartments, and Ruth and Gloria settled in upstairs. Rats shared their space and kept them

Gloria and her mother lived in several Eastern cities before moving to Toledo, Ohio.

Gloria (front) attended summer camp in Michigan, which gave her a brief respite from her caregiving duties.

awake at night with their scratching in the walls. Once, Gloria was bitten by a rat, and Ruth took her to the emergency room to have the wound treated. But it was rare for Ruth to be able to act like a mother. Ruth's mental condition continued to worsen, and Gloria was forced to run the house, as well as care for her unstable mother. In later life, Gloria said:

*For many years, I … never imagined my
mother any way other than … someone to
be worried about and cared for; an invalid
who lay in bed with eyes closed and lips
moving in occasional response to voices
only she could hear.*

Books offered Gloria a temporary escape from
the role of caregiver. She enjoyed *Little Women* and
Gone with the Wind. She also read Nancy Drew
mysteries. Gloria continued to tap dance, as well. One
summer, she danced in operettas, sometimes earning
$10 a night. She and her mother sorely needed the
income her dancing provided. Gloria practiced over
and over—much to the distress of other people in
the house. Tap dancing, however, offered her only
temporary pleasure. Ruth's condition grew ever
worse, and Gloria saw no long-term relief from her
caregiving duties.

Gloria attended junior high at Toledo's Raymer
Junior High School and high school at Waite High
School. Gloria made many friends, and she held after-
school jobs that allowed her to stay away from home.
She sold clothing in a store and read scripts and spun
records at a radio station. She even worked as a
magician's assistant. But she continued to be bound
by her mother's need for care. Gloria recalled that her
mother's condition sometimes embarrassed her:

[She] woke in the early dark, too frightened and disoriented to remember that I was at my usual after-school job, and so called the police to find me. Humiliated in front of my friends ... I would yell at her—and she would bow her head in fear and say, "I'm sorry, I'm sorry, I'm sorry," just as she had done so often when my otherwise-kind-hearted father had yelled at her in frustration. Perhaps the worst thing about suffering is that it finally hardens the hearts of those around it.

Gloria attended Toledo's Waite High School through her junior year.

Gloria continued to find relief in dancing. She

took ballet lessons and performed during junior concerts with the Toledo Orchestra. She became friends with an African-American girl in her ballet class. The girl was her first black friend, and their relationship helped Gloria understand the vital difference between race and class.

Gloria had become very aware of class differences during her time in Toledo. She felt that the women in her working-class neighborhood had little to look forward to. In later life, she said, "Class was very important to me and what I became. Neighborhood women were clearly divided into victims and nice girls, and if you became a victim, not a nice girl, your life was over."

When Gloria was 17 years old, with one year left of high school, she was presented with an opportunity that would change her life dramatically. Her sister, Susanne, lived in Washington, D.C., and she invited Gloria to move in with her. Gloria had found a way out of Toledo. She could finish high school in Washington, D.C.—if she could find someone to care for her mother. Gloria and Susanne talked with their father. After much coaxing, Leo agreed to take care of Ruth, but only for a year. He said, "All right, but one year is all. We're synchronizing our watches." Gloria's childhood had been swallowed up by the early responsibility of taking care of her mother. Now, on the edge of adulthood, she was finally free to live life for herself.

Gloria packed up and moved to Washington, D.C. Unlike her high school in Toledo, Western High School focused on preparing students for college. Gloria's world expanded quickly. She made many friends and was elected vice president of her senior class. She was a good high school student but not a great one. She was quick-witted and imaginative, but she did not do very well on her College Board test.

Washington, D.C., the nation's capital, was a new and exciting environment for Gloria.

She applied to Cornell and Stanford universities, but both rejected her. After a Western High School counselor wrote her a recommendation letter, however, she was accepted at Smith College, where her sister had gone. Going there would be a big step toward a better future—if she could come up with the money. Fortunately, Ruth had sold the family home in Toledo the previous year, before moving to California to be cared for by Leo. The money from the sale was set aside to pay for Gloria's tuition at Smith. Gloria's college adventure was about to begin. ℘

Smith College in Northampton, Massachusetts, was founded in 1871 by Sophia Smith. She felt women could gain power through education and wanted them to have a place where they could learn valuable skills. Today, Smith is the largest private liberal arts college for women in the United States.

4 COLLEGE AND BEYOND

Chapter

cx/x/o

When Gloria arrived at Smith College, her mother, who had returned from her year in Leo's care, was arriving at a hospital in Baltimore, Maryland. There, Ruth was treated for an anxiety disorder, and her condition eventually improved somewhat.

Gloria loved college from the moment she arrived. She felt she had finally found a home. After so many years of being a caregiver, she was pleased to finally be able to relax. She had a clean dormitory to live in, and she was fed on a regular schedule. Gloria wondered why so many of her classmates seemed so eager to marry when it meant leaving such a comfortable and welcoming place.

Though she made many friends with the young women she met at Smith, Gloria found the

---

Gloria felt transformed by her time in India. While there, she darkened her hair and dressed in Indian clothing.

In the United States in the 1950s, more women began to attend college, but the opportunities available to them after graduation were still limited. Most women worked in low-paying secretarial or service jobs, and once they married, they were expected to quit working, stay home, and raise children.

experiences she brought with her to be very different from those of her classmates. Many of her friends at Smith came from wealthy backgrounds and not only had doting parents but also servants to tend to their needs. At first, Gloria was embarrassed and disliked talking with them about her childhood, but she soon learned to turn her early troubles into amusing stories that entertained her friends.

Gloria also found ways to use her unusual background to her advantage. Through years of caring for her mother, she had developed many useful skills that many of her Smith friends did not have. Gloria was able to trade her skills and services for those of others, so that a lesson to a privileged classmate on how to iron a dress got her a lesson on French grammar in return.

At Smith, Gloria was free from the many responsibilities she had shouldered in junior high and high school, and she was able to concentrate fully on her studies. Her grades began to improve. She also developed an interest in international politics, and she decided to major in government. It was

this interest that prompted her to pursue a chance to study in Europe. In 1954, she entered a program called Junior Year Abroad, which allowed college

Smith is the nation's largest liberal arts college for women.

students to study in France, Italy, Switzerland, or Spain. First, she went to France and brushed up on her French by living with a family in Paris. Then, she set off for Geneva, Switzerland. At the University of Geneva, Gloria studied history, law, and literature from an international perspective. After the year was up, she received a scholarship that allowed her to spend the summer studying politics and literature at Oxford University in England.

Somehow, Gloria found time for a boyfriend in her busy schedule. After returning to the United States in 1955, a friend set Gloria up on a blind date with Blair Chotzinoff, a young Air National Guard pilot. Gloria had dated other men while in college, but Blair was special. He cared deeply for Gloria. He even rented a plane and wrote her name in the sky above campus. It wasn't long before the couple was engaged.

On June 3, 1956, Gloria graduated with honors from Smith College. Leo, Ruth, and Susanne were there to celebrate her achievement. But the commencement address offended Gloria and other Smith graduates by identifying their worth and their future as dependent on the men they would marry. Though she was engaged to Blair, Gloria had decided that marriage was not for her. In fact, she had accepted a scholarship to leave the country for a year of study in India. She wanted to put some more distance between herself and her mother, but

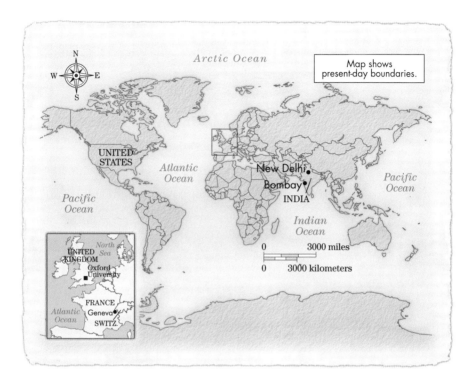

Map shows present-day boundaries.

Gloria studied on three of the seven continents.

most of all, she was afraid that if she stayed in the United States, she would end up marrying Blair. She returned Blair's engagement ring and planned her trip to India.

First, Gloria flew to London, England, and stayed with friends while she waited for her visa. While in London, Gloria found out she was pregnant. Gloria strongly believed marriage and motherhood were not right for her at the time. She struggled with a difficult decision. Though she could not have known it at the time, her choice would one day come to determine the course of her career.

Abortion was illegal in the United States at the time, but it could be legally performed in England if two doctors gave their signed permission. Gloria found two doctors to sign the papers, and one of them—a woman—performed the procedure. Afterward, Gloria felt very isolated and alone. For a time, she fell into depression. While she continued to be troubled by the experience, she resolved to continue her studies. When her visa finally came, Gloria set out for India.

On February 4, 1957, Gloria arrived in the Indian city of Bombay. From there she traveled to New Delhi, where she enrolled at the University of Delhi with Kayla Achter, a classmate from Smith. After the three-month term had ended, she and Kayla traveled together for a short time, but Gloria soon realized that she wanted to learn much more. She was especially interested in the nonviolent approach to oppression practiced by followers of Mohandas Gandhi, an Indian spiritual and political leader who had helped his country win independence from the British in 1947.

In the early 1900s, India was part of the British Empire. Indian lawyer Mohandas Gandhi helped free India from British control by using a unique method of nonviolent protest. He is honored by the people of India as the father of their nation. Gandhi lived a simple life and thought it was wrong to kill animals for food or clothing. His followers called Gandhi the Mahatma, which means "Great Soul." Gandhi was killed by an assassin in January 1948.

In southern India, a group of Gandhi's followers organized a walk to protest the caste, or class, riots. Gloria joined them. She had darkened her hair and begun to dress like a traditional Indian woman, wearing a loose-fitting wrap-around sari and sandals.

Gloria attended classes at the University of Delhi, in India's capital city.

Gloria and the other walkers traveled from village to village asking rich landowners to donate land to the poor. Many dusty walks took as many

Indians think of Mohandas Gandhi as the father of their nation.

as 13 hours a day. People in the villages fed the walkers enough to keep them going. At night, they slept on woven mats in the villages. During the cool mornings they sat and talked to the villagers. Gloria enjoyed speaking to the people she met along the way.

As she traveled throughout the country, Gloria

closely observed Indian society. She noticed that women and members of the lower castes were oppressed. The gap between the rich and the poor was so large that she could not imagine how it could possibly be bridged. She began to think of her own country in a new way, and she wrote articles about the views she was beginning to develop. She was also developing a talent for writing, and in 1957, before leaving India, she wrote *The Thousand Indias* to be used as a guidebook for the Indian Tourist Bureau.

Gloria returned to the United States a changed woman. She wrote, "Most of us have a few events that divide our lives into 'before' and 'after.' This was one for me." With her return, Gloria left behind a world of poor people for one rich with belongings. She thought the United States seemed like an "enormous frosted cupcake in the middle of a million starving people."

An Indian myth tells how the caste system came about. Brahma, a spiritual leader, made a man from clay. The whole man represented Indian society. Each caste came from part of the clay man's body. High caste members were called Brahmans. They came from the mouth. Under them were rulers and warriors molded from the arms. From the thighs came merchants and people who owned land. The feet brought forth artisans and servants. "Untouchables" earned their name from the work they do. They completed jobs such as cleaning bathrooms or hard labor. While the government today frowns upon the caste system, some people still support it.

5 A YOUNG WRITER

e∕∿∿ও

Gloria Steinem was brimming with ideas when she arrived back in the United States. She wanted to share them, through her writing skills, to improve the lives of others.

She traveled to New York City in search of a job at a newspaper, but it was difficult at that time for women to find rewarding work. Steinem interviewed for a position at the *Saturday Review* and applied to the India Committee of the Asian Society, but she was turned down at both places. Finally, Clive Gray, an American she had met in India, offered her a job. She moved to Cambridge, Massachusetts, to do public relations work for the Independent Research Service, an educational foundation funded by the Central Intelligence Agency (CIA). This foundation

Gloria Steinem left court after testifying about her Playboy bunny article.

sent American students to international communist youth festivals. There, these Americans would promote democratic ideals throughout the world.

Steinem did her job well and was known as a hard worker. But after the 1959 Youth Festival in Vienna,

Crowds gathered in front of Vienna's city hall during the 1959 World Youth Festival.

Austria, ended, she once again needed to look for work. She met with Harvey Kurtzman, the publisher of *Mad* magazine. Kurtzman was ready to publish a new political satire magazine called *Help! For Tired Minds.* He offered her a job as an editorial assistant arranging interviews with celebrities. But Steinem longed to write about the things she found important, and she continued to pursue other work.

She was offered a job writing for the men's magazine *Esquire.* A few of her articles focused on dating in New York City and cooking for men who did not want to cook. She wrote humorous articles and was good at giving advice.

Steinem's life was going well. She was beginning to find success as a writer, and she enjoyed spending time with her many new friends. But on April 20, 1961, tragedy struck. Leo Steinem was injured in a car accident in California. Steinem rushed to be with him, but he died before she arrived. Steinem grieved her loss. Though they had not had much contact since her parents' divorce, she had greatly admired her father. He had allowed her to become an independent and intelligent person and had honored her by respecting her thoughts and opinions.

Steinem continued to receive more and more writing assignments. Her articles appeared in *The New York Times* and magazines such as *Glamour* and *Harper's*. Her articles on actor Paul Newman and singer Barbra Streisand were published in *Ladies' Home Journal*. She did a feature on TV newswoman Barbara Walters and wrote a concert booklet on folksingers Peter, Paul, and Mary.

"I Was a Playboy Bunny," her 1963 piece in *Show*, caused a disturbance with the reading public. She received threatening phone calls and was the subject of several lawsuits. The piece gave her almost overnight fame, but it was not the kind of fame she sought. People questioned whether a beautiful woman could be a serious writer.

But writing—especially about important issues—is what Steinem most wanted to do. She later said:

> *Writing is the only thing that passes the three tests ... first, when I'm doing it, I don't feel that I should be doing something else; second, it produces a sense of accomplishment and, once in a while, pride; and third, it's frightening.*

By 1965, Steinem was very much in demand as a writer. She had begun writing for *That Was the Week That Was*, an irreverent television overview of weekly world news. But even though she had gained financial security, she still chased acceptance as a serious writer.

In April 1968, Steinem's *Esquire* co-worker Clay Felker left the magazine to found one of his own.

Steinem was among the group that helped him make the new magazine a reality. Steinem became a contributing editor and political columnist for *New York* magazine. She could finally write the kind of serious articles she had dreamed about. She wrote, "For the first time, I wasn't writing about one thing while caring about something else."

Steinem soon became known as a political activist. Her column, "The City Politic," helped bring

Clay Felker was an important figure in the development of Steinem's career.

attention to issues she felt were important. She wrote about the Vietnam War, the plight of migrant farm-workers, the living conditions of poor people, and the rights of women. In her column, she expressed her support for presidential candidate Eugene McCarthy, who was running on a strong antiwar platform. Steinem agreed to cover McCarthy's campaign for the magazine, but she felt uncomfortable about how

In the early 1970s, Steinem (at home with cat Crazy Alice) was eager to find an outlet for her political views.

women involved with the campaign were perceived. She later wrote:

> *Like other women, I had either stayed at the edges doing menial jobs or been hidden away in some backroom because (a) it might be counterproductive to admit that a female was working on speeches or policy decisions, and (b) if she was under 60 ... someone might think she was having an affair with the candidate.*

George McGovern entered the presidential race in August 1968, and Steinem backed his candidacy over McCarthy's. She raised money and handled publicity for his campaign. She even advised McGovern on what to wear.

Later that August, the Democratic National Convention was held in Chicago, Illinois. War protesters, police, and military troops clashed outside the convention hall. Police made more than 500 arrests, and about 100 police and 100 protesters were injured.

In 1954, the Asian nation of Vietnam was split in two. North Vietnam had a communist government. The communist leaders of the Soviet Union supported North Vietnam's efforts to take over South Vietnam. The United States opposed the spread of communism and began sending military aid to South Vietnam. By 1965, the United States was actively fighting to keep South Vietnam out of communist hands. As many as 500,000 U.S. troops served in Asia at one time, and more than 58,000 were killed. Protests against the war influenced President Richard Nixon's decision to pull most U.S. troops out of Vietnam in 1973. Two years later, North Vietnam won the Vietnam War.

Steinem was unharmed, but her glasses were broken in a shoving match. When the convention ended, Minnesota Senator Hubert Humphrey, not McGovern, had won the Democratic Party's nomination. In November 1968, Humphrey lost to Richard M. Nixon. The war in Vietnam would continue.

Antiwar sentiment continued to build, and peace supporters conducted many rallies. Steinem regularly covered the events. Her time in India had taught her to believe in peaceful means of resolving disputes, and she continued to publicly declare her opposition to the war. She made her own peaceful protest

Protesters rallied against the Vietnam War in New York City's Central Park in 1968.

against the way the government was using public tax dollars. The U.S. government used 10 percent of the income tax people paid to fund the war in Vietnam. Steinem and other writers and editors opposed to the war employed what was called the Writers and Editors War Tax Protest. They simply held back 10 percent of the income tax that they should have paid.

In the late 1960s, Steinem covered the migrant workers' union, United Farm Workers, for a story. Cesar Chavez, the group's leader, was persuasive. Steinem had long ago established a pattern of helping the underdog, and she took up the migrant workers' cause, helping them raise funds and joining them in protest marches. Her articles in *Life*, *Time*, and *Look* magazines brought their plight to the public. Steinem was writing about what she believed in and was helping to make a difference.

In the 1960s, migrant workers did much of the farm work in the Southwest. But they received low pay, spent too much time in the field, and had poor housing. They also had few rest breaks, were exposed to dangerous pesticides, and lacked toilets in the fields. Cesar Chavez became the workers' outspoken leader. Chavez admired the work of Gandhi just as Gloria Steinem did. He fought to organize the farmworkers and win better conditions. The United Farm Workers was born.

6 FINDING FEMINISM

ᴄ~ᴗᴗ~ᴗ

The women's movement was also a cause that had captured Steinem's attention. She was familiar with Betty Friedan, a feminist who had come to public attention with her book, *The Feminine Mystique*, which focused on issues of educated middle-class homemakers. In 1966, Friedan had helped found the National Organization for Women (NOW). This organization's goal was to make women more active participants in society, so women could achieve equal rights with men.

Friedan was at the head of what is known as the second wave of feminism. The first wave began in 1848, when early feminists met in Seneca Falls, New York, for the first-ever meeting on women's rights. The organizers had drafted a Declaration of Sentiments,

With the publication of The Feminine Mystique, *Betty Friedan (center) became a leader of the second wave of feminism.*

based on the U.S. Declaration of Independence, and 68 women and 32 men signed the document in support. The declaration called for women's suffrage, or the right to vote. But it took many years to win that right. In 1920, the 19th Amendment to the U.S. Constitution finally gave women the right to vote.

An 1869 political cartoon shows what many felt about women in the suffrage movement.

Once women achieved suffrage, they turned their attention to other issues, such as equal pay for equal work, domestic violence, and reproductive freedom. NOW was one of the most prominent organizations

of this second wave of feminism. Steinem knew that NOW was very important, but she felt the organization did not represent the full range of feminists. Most NOW members were upper- and middle-class white women. Steinem sympathized with members of NOW, but she did not identify with them. They did not represent her background. Steinem believed that to be successful, the feminist movement also had to include younger and more radical females. She did not realize the important role she would soon play in revitalizing the cause.

On March 21, 1969, *New York* magazine assigned Steinem to cover a rally put on by a radical feminist group, the Redstockings. She attended the rally in search of a story, but instead she found her life's work. As she later said, "[I]t wasn't until I went to cover a local abortion hearing for *New York* that the politics of my own life began to explain my interests."

> *The name* Redstockings *came from combining* bluestockings, *a 19th-century term for educated or strong-minded women, with* red, *which refers to social consciousness.*

The rally was held to protest the official hearing on New York's abortion laws, which the Redstockings felt was handled improperly. At that time, abortions in the United States were illegal. Women who had one anyway took a large health risk, and complications sometimes led to death. But many women at the rally had endured an abortion and talked openly about their own experiences.

Steinem's past abortion had made her feel isolated and alone. At the rally, she realized that others shared her feelings. She later wrote about the experience:

> Suddenly I was not learning intellectually what was wrong. I knew. I had sought and endured an abortion when I was newly out of college, but told no one. If one in three or four adult women shared this experience, why [was] each of us made to feel criminal and alone?

And then she wondered further, "How much power could we ever have if we had no power over the fate of our own bodies?"

From that point forward, no one thought of Steinem without the word *feminist*. She wholeheartedly committed herself to the cause and became one of women's rights' most outspoken champions. But for her first truly feminist article, Steinem paired her new interest with an old one. In "After Black Power, Women's Liberation," Steinem explained the natural alliance between civil rights and women's rights. She wrote that if the two movements supported each other, both would succeed. The article won the prestigious 1970

Young African-Americans raised their fists in the Black Power salute.

Penney-Missouri Journalism Award.

Steinem supported the women's movement through her writing, but she was nervous about standing up and giving a speech in public. In the end, however, her desire to spread the word was stronger than her fear of public speaking, and in September 1969, she spoke to the Women's National Democratic Club about her prize-winning article. Steinem enlisted the help of her friend Dorothy Pittman Hughes as a speaking partner. Hughes had roots in the civil rights movement, and she ran a child-care center in New York City. She had an easy, comfortable way of speaking, and her presence helped ease Steinem's discomfort.

The civil rights movement of the 1950s and 1960s was influential in spurring women to rebel against traditional roles. An African-American woman, Rosa Parks, sparked the movement when she refused to give up her bus seat to a white man.

Lawyer and social activist Florynce Kennedy was another of Steinem's speaking partners. The pair spoke in big cities, small towns, and out in the country. At the time, there were few speakers spreading the word about feminism, but together Steinem and Kennedy touched "every state but Alaska." Author Margaret Sloan became Steinem's third speaking partner. Only in her 20s, Sloan brought a youthful voice to the cause.

All three of Steinem's speaking partners were African-American women, and their presence helped Steinem attract an audience beyond the white, upper-middle-class women who were the movement's original targets. Together, Steinem and her partners presented an inclusive and hopeful feminist message. "My daughter will be what I never could have been," said a woman who heard Steinem speak.

On a spring day in May 1970, Steinem spoke in front of the U.S. Senate in support of the Equal Rights Amendment (ERA). The amendment, which was first proposed in 1923 as an amendment to the U.S. Constitution, would give equal rights to both men and women. Its text states, "Equality of rights under the law shall not be denied or abridged by the

United States or by any state on account of sex." The amendment had been brought before Congress each session beginning in 1923, but it had never passed.

Steinem gave a compelling testimony. She said women were excluded from many things. They could be refused service in a restaurant or be turned down if they wanted to rent an apartment. She told

Women rallied in front of the White House in support of the ERA and against the war in Vietnam.

> Feminist Alice Paul (1885–1977) drafted the Equal Rights Amendment (ERA) in 1923. She was one of the first American leaders of the movement for equal rights for women. In 1913, she founded the National Woman's Party, which supported equal rights for women. She worked with international women's organizations in the 1930s and founded the World Woman's Party in 1938.

Congress, "I have been denied a society in which women are encouraged, or even allowed, to think of themselves as first class citizens and responsible human beings." Steinem wanted myths about women's place in society to change. She stated, "We are changing our own consciousness, and that of the country." But doing so was not easy.

Conservative Phyllis Schlafly opposed the ERA. She worried that taxpayers would end up paying for abortions and argued that passage of the ERA would bring about weaker punishment for sex crimes against women. Others were concerned that the ERA would mean unisex bathrooms for all and that women would be drafted as soldiers. But feminist leaders argued that they simply wanted the same pay for men and women who performed the same jobs.

Steinem's own mother would probably have supported the ERA and other feminist causes if they had been organized during her younger days. Before Ruth married, she worked as a newspaper reporter and a math teacher. Eventually, the stress of fulfilling the traditional roles of wife and mother

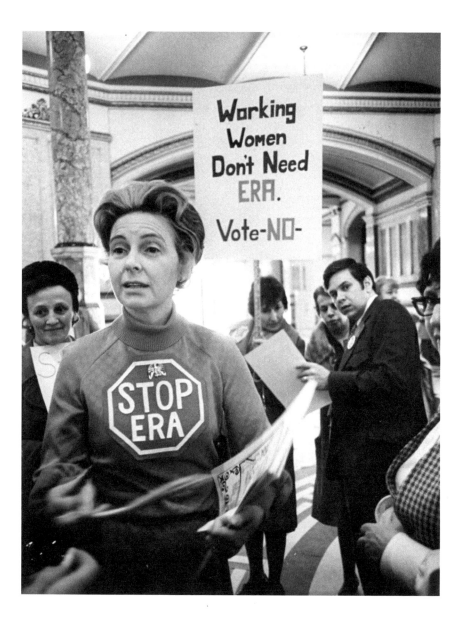

while maintaining a career became too great, and she suffered a mental breakdown. Later in life, however, the spirit that had allowed her to hold those jobs

Phyllis Schlafly and other conservatives rallied against the ERA.

emerged again. Steinem recalled that her mother often showed "flashes of a different woman inside; one with a wry kind of humor, a sense of adventure, and a love of learning."

Steinem and her mother maintained a close relationship throughout Ruth's life.

Ruth was well enough to live alone during most of her last 20 years of life. Despite Steinem's busy schedule, she was her mother's frequent companion during those years. They took yearly trips together. Ruth was supportive of her daughter's work, but that did not prevent her from using a false name when she visited her women's club.

On August 26, 1970, Steinem, Friedan, and other leaders in NOW planned a peaceful demonstration in honor of the passage of the 19th amendment to the Constitution, which had given women the right to vote. They called their event the Women's Strike for Equality. Other groups, such as the Redstockings, the Young Women's Christian Association (YWCA), and the New York Radical Feminists, joined in. Women who months before had been satisfied with "their place" in the world joined the demonstration as well. The women's movement was picking up speed. Society would never be the same. ℘

After years of controversy, Congress finally passed the ERA in 1972, but it had to be ratified by the states within seven years. An extension in 1978 changed the deadline to 1982, but at that time, only 35 states of the necessary 38 states had ratified the amendment. Though it has been reintroduced a number of times since then, it has failed to pass.

7 SPEAKING FOR WOMEN

❧✦❧

In 1971, Smith College invited Steinem to address the graduating class. The speech she delivered, "The Politics of Women," lashed out at the college for which she had once felt such warm feelings. She criticized Smith for failing to honor women in history and for supporting conservative ideas about women in society. She went on to talk about housework as "the only work that is only noticed if you don't do it" and declare illegal abortions to be "the number one health problem among women." She urged students to change society and challenged Smith to become a feminist institution.

Steinem's address divided the audience. While the graduates applauded her ideas, many of the older listeners were upset and offended. Half of the parents

Pat Carbine (left) and Gloria Steinem co-founded Ms. *magazine, a unique publication that was owned and run entirely by women.*

attending walked out. Today, few people would be offended by her ideas, but in 1971, her comments were scandalous and daring. One listener wrote a letter claiming "Filth is filth."

Harvard University also invited Steinem to speak at its formal *Harvard Law Review* banquet. Instead of making the usual general comments, Steinem referred to specific problems and gave concrete solutions to fix them. Though this speech was again met with both applause and silence, in time, changes were made in the treatment of women at Harvard Law School.

Steinem had become the most prominent speaker in the feminist movement. She was a celebrity. *Vogue* and *Redbook* magazines featured articles on her life. On August 16, 1971, her face flashed across national newsstands on the cover of *Newsweek* magazine. Two months later, *Esquire* ran an article about her called "She: The Awesome Power of Gloria Steinem."

In 1971, Steinem and other feminist leaders pooled their efforts to form the National Women's

> *Steinem had become friends with attorney Brenda Feigen after Feigen invited her to testify before Congress on the Equal Rights Amendment (ERA) in 1970. When Steinem wavered over accepting the invitation to speak at the Harvard banquet, Feigen remembered the discrimination she had felt as a female student there and convinced Steinem to deliver the scathing address. Steinem and Feigen went on to work together on many feminist projects.*

Political Caucus (NWPC). Among the group's founders were Betty Friedan, the author of *The Feminine Mystique*, Shirley Chisholm, the first African-American woman elected to the House of Representatives, and Bella Abzug, a congresswoman from New York. This organization backed women in bids for public office. Out of this group was born the Women's Action Alliance (WAA). The WAA helped abused women and those treated unfairly at work. The group also tried to change textbooks that

Steinem (right) and other keynote speakers prepared at the opening of a NWPC event in 1971.

BETTY SMITH

DOROTHY HEIGHT

favored mostly males.

Though Steinem's recent fame had come from her organizing and speaking, she still thought of herself primarily as a writer. But in 1971, there was little market for the kind of feminist pieces she wanted to write. Most magazines for women dealt with raising children, housekeeping, marriage, or makeup. If Steinem wanted to write serious feminist pieces, she would have to create her own opportunity.

Steinem held a series of informal meetings with other female writers to talk about starting a new magazine. Many of them felt they had long been muzzled by a publishing world hostile to their ideas. They were eager to work with Steinem on a feminist publication. Pleased at the show of support, Steinem decided to make it happen.

In late 1971, Steinem's dream became a reality. With help from *New York* magazine founder Clay Felker and members of his editorial staff, she was able to slip a short sample issue of the new feminist magazine inside the December year-end issue of *New York* as a "one-shot" test. The magazine was

Although it was Steinem's dream to see a feminist magazine, she was always somewhat uncomfortable with her role. She later said, "The magazine was something I wanted to happen; I wanted there to be a feminist magazine, but I didn't want to do it. I remember saying ... 'I'll do this for two years, no longer.'"

called *Ms.*, after a form of address for women that did not require knowledge of their marital status.

The magazine had a dramatic and immediate effect on all who read it. It featured articles with titles such as "The Housewife's Moment of Truth," "My Mother the Dentist," "Raising Kids Without Sex Roles," and "Welfare Is a Woman's Issue." The 300,000 copies of the premier issue, which came out in January 1972, sold out in just eight days. Within weeks, 26,000 subscription orders were placed.

Many women worked to make Ms. *magazine important and successful.*

Though *Ms.* was welcomed by many in the United

States, it was not without its critics. News anchor Harry Reasoner thought that the magazine would run out of things to say within six months. Many thought the magazine was too radical and undermined society's structure with its feminist message. Others from within the women's movement, however, thought that *Ms.* was too mainstream. They believed that in trying to achieve a broad audience, Steinem and her staff had toned down their feminist beliefs.

One of the issues that continually troubled Steinem was finding appropriate advertisers for the magazine. She wanted to include advertisements beyond the usual makeup and other beauty products. She worked hard to get a variety of ads, including many for products such as cars and computers that were not usually displayed in women's magazines. It proved difficult, however, to attract ads usually reserved for a male audience, especially for a feminist magazine. At one point, the cosmetics company Revlon pulled its ad from the magazine because the women on the cover of *Ms.* were not wearing any makeup—despite the fact that these women were Russian feminist protesters and the photo accompanied an award-winning article. Such issues eventually prompted *Ms.* to become ad-free in 1990.

Despite difficulties with advertisers, the magazine continued to be a success with readers. Steinem began to look for new ways to help her cause. In 1972, she and her co-workers at *Ms.* began the *Ms.* Foundation for Women. At the time, no organizations gave money to women's causes, and Steinem wanted

In 1973, actress Marlo Thomas produced the popular television program Free to Be ... You and Me to benefit the Ms. Foundation for Women. This popular program won an Emmy award and continues to raise money today through book and recording sales.

to do something useful with the profits from the magazine. The *Ms.* Foundation raises and gives money to projects that help women and girls. Foundation programs encourage self-esteem and self-expression. As Steinem herself wrote, "Believing a true self is what allows a true self to be born."

Over the years, the *Ms.* Foundation has funded many important projects. Perhaps the most well known of these is Take Our Daughters to Work Day, in which girls are introduced to the workplace and all the options that are available to them.

The year the *Ms.* Foundation began, something radical happened in politics. Shirley Chisholm, a congresswoman from New York and a founding member of the NWPC, ran for president of the United States. She was the first African-American ever to run for the position. Many believed Steinem would support Chisholm, but as she had in 1968, she supported George McGovern. Though she later publicly supported Chisholm and even wrote a speech Chisholm delivered on television, Steinem's double backing confused both the candidates and the public.

Steinem's increasing fame gave special weight to these public shows of political support. With the popularity of *Ms.* and her continuing presence as a speaker and writer, Steinem's name and face had become synonymous with the women's movement. She was featured in articles in magazines such as *Newsweek*, *People*, and *Time*. *McCall's*, a traditional women's magazine that had originally been led by *Ms.* co-founder Pat Carbine, named Steinem its Woman of the Year in 1972. That same year, Steinem

In January 1972, Shirley Chisholm announced her groundbreaking campaign for president of the United States.

was invited to speak at the National Press Club in Washington, D.C., not long after it allowed women members. She was the first woman ever to address this organization, and they jokingly gave her a tie to mark the occasion.

As her star continued to rise, Steinem remained a strong force in the Democratic Party. She represented the NWPC as a delegate at the 1972 Democratic Convention. Her selection as a delegate—and her

Gloria Steinem spoke as a delegate at the 1972 Democratic National Convention.

increasingly prominent role as a spokesperson for feminism—turned some of the movement's founders against her. Betty Friedan had long felt that Steinem was the subject of too much attention. Friedan began making unflattering comments about Steinem to reporters. The Redstockings, the group whose rally had prompted Steinem's involvement in the feminist movement, turned against her as well. They claimed she was taking focus away from their group and that her views weren't radical enough. They also made charges about Steinem's involvement with the CIA, which had now taken on an unsavory reputation, when she worked on the youth festivals in the 1950s.

Members of the movement were beginning to fight among themselves over issues as well. Differences of opinion on abortion rights and other important topics began to divide feminists. The women's movement remained a powerful force, but it was beginning to show signs of wear. ℘

8 CREATING A POSITIVE WORLD

Chapter

❧⟨✕⟩❧

By the late 1970s, women's rights had begun to gain attention as an international issue. The United Nations declared 1975 to be International Women's Year. Two years later, U.S. President Jimmy Carter formed an International Women's Year commission that would organize a national conference of women. The commission was led by Congresswoman Bella Abzug, who had helped found the NWPC earlier that decade. Steinem and a number of other prominent female leaders were elected to serve as well.

The National Women's Conference was held in Houston, Texas, in November 1977. To open the historic gathering, women runners carried a torch 2,610 miles (4,180 km) from Seneca Falls, New York, site of the first women's rights convention,

Gloria Steinem signed copies of her book Moving Beyond Words *at its publication in 1994.*

Coretta Scott King, wife of slain civil rights leader Martin Luther King Jr., spoke at the National Women's Conference.

to Houston.

The three-day National Women's Conference brought together women from a tremendous variety of backgrounds and with a similarly wide variety of issues to address. But despite competing priorities, women at the conference were able to make important progress on 26 different issues. For Steinem, the conference proved that women working together could achieve great things. She later wrote, "Houston and all the events surrounding it [became] a landmark in personal history, the sort of milestone that divides our sense of time. ... Was it before or after Houston?"

Steinem had expressed similar feelings after her year in India, so perhaps it is fitting that around that time she returned to India to visit women's groups in Bombay, New Delhi, and Ahmedabad. What she found surprised her. As one Indian woman said, "We can't read, but we can think." Thoughts led to action, action led to change, and the status of women in India began to improve dramatically.

In 1982, New York magazine published its list of the nation's most influential women. Steinem shared the fifth-place spot with Phyllis Schlafly, the conservative she had battled over the ERA. Other top 10 picks included the first woman Supreme Court justice, Sandra Day O'Connor, and Eleanor Smeal, president of NOW.

Much of the progress came from the work of a woman named Ela Bhatt. A lawyer and labor organizer in the mold of Mohandas Gandhi, Bhatt used peaceful protests to bring about change. Women in India wanted better working conditions and safe day-care places for their children. They also wanted higher wages for items they handcrafted and sold. Bhatt worked as an advocate for Indian women. She helped found the Self-Employed Women's Association, an organization that encouraged women to work together to improve their circumstances. When Steinem visited India in

Activist Ela Bhatt helped improve the condition of women in her home country, India.

1978, Bhatt's work on behalf of women was showing signs of real progress.

In 1982, *Ms.* magazine turned 10 years old. When Steinem began the magazine, she never expected the success it would have—or that she would still be involved 10 years later. Rightly proud of their achievement, Steinem and her colleagues celebrated with an anniversary party on June 4 in New York City. The 10th anniversary edition of *Ms.* celebrated as well, honoring the achievements women had made since the magazine's founding.

In 1983, Steinem published *Outrageous Acts and Everyday Rebellions*, which quickly became a best-seller. The book was a collection of some of her past essays, including her well-known article, "I Was a Playboy Bunny." She also included a powerful essay about her mother, "Ruth's Song (Because She Could Not Sing It)." Ruth had died in 1981, and Steinem found it difficult to lose a parent for whom she herself had played the role of mother. Of Ruth's life and death, she wrote:

> *Dying seems less sad than having lived too little. But at least we're now asking questions about all the Ruths in all our family mysteries. If her song inspires that, I think she would be the first to say: It was worth the singing.*

In 1986, Steinem discovered a lump in her breast

Another party, in 1984, celebrated Steinem's 50th birthday. Many important women attended the event, including women who had influenced Steinem, such as civil rights activist Rosa Parks, and women who had benefited from Steinem's work, such as astronaut Sally Ride.

In 1986, Steinem published a biography of 1950s movie star Marilyn Monroe. She wrote the book primarily to raise money so that she could pay back her publisher for a favor he had done her. But she was also interested in Monroe because the actress had lived many of the traditional female experiences that Steinem had spent her career fighting against.

during a routine medical checkup. The diagnosis was cancer. She thought, "So this is how it's all going to end," and then, "I've had a wonderful life." She says that "acceptance may sound odd, but I felt those words in every last cell of my being. It was a moment I won't forget." She was 52 years old. Much of Steinem's adult life had been spent fighting for a cause. She used the same fighting spirit to battle cancer.

Steinem underwent surgery to remove the lump, followed by six weeks of radiation treatment. The treatment was successful. At first, she did not publicly acknowledge her battle with cancer, and in fact she was treated under the name of her grandmother, Marie Ochs. It wasn't until 1988 that Steinem spoke publicly about her experience. She remains cancer-free today.

During this time, Steinem thought a lot about her life. She was continually exhausted from traveling around the world for writing assignments and speaking engagements. Her day-to-day life was not well organized. Many boxes cluttered her home. Unpacking her belongings meant settling down, something she had never been allowed to do during

Steinem (left) and Pat Carbine celebrated 15 years of Ms. *magazine in 1987.*

her childhood. She began to realize that her unsettled childhood was continuing to influence her adult life. So in 1986, she met with a counselor who helped her work through feelings about her youth. The counseling sessions helped her look inside herself and open up more to others. They allowed her to connect with her own past and move on.

Steinem's experience with counseling helped her develop new attitudes and skills she wanted other women to know about. In 1992, she wrote *Revolution from Within: A Book of Self-Esteem*. This collection of essays offers readers self-help and inspirational ideas. Steinem offers guidance on how people can use their past to shape the future.

In 1993, Steinem was inducted into the National Women's Hall of Fame. She was recognized for her contributions to society in many different fields, but Steinem felt her work was still far from complete. The following year, she published another book. *Moving Beyond Words* addresses Steinem's views on publishing, advertising, and society in general. Steinem turned 60 years old that year, and she wrote about the experience in a chapter called "Doing Sixty." She wrote that "fifty felt like leaving a much-loved and familiar country … but sixty feels like arriving at the border of a new one."

In 1995, Steinem and Andrea Johnston, a California teacher, created a special study program called Girls Speak Out. Johnston's book *Girls Speak Out* was written as a guide to help girls when they find it difficult to voice their opinion. Johnston felt that girls need to "share their truths as a path to self-esteem—that seems to be the only way we find out that we're not alone in our experiences, and that together, we can change them for the better." In the program Steinem helped create, girls from age 9 to 19 meet together and follow plans from the book. The program is funded by the *Ms.* Foundation for Women.

While the foundation backed important feminist

causes, the magazine continued to put out issue after issue. Steinem had gradually become less involved, and the magazine changed hands several times over the years. In 2001, the Feminist Majority Foundation, a women's action and research group, took over the magazine. Under their ownership, the magazine turned 30 years old in 2002. *Ms.* readers had carried their hope for equality straight into the new millennium. ✍

The program Girls Speak Out helps girls learn to value their opinions and make their voices heard.

9 THE NEW MILLENNIUM

ᶜ⤳✕⤳ᵉ

*D*uring her life, Gloria Steinem had enjoyed many long-term relationships with men. She and most of the men remained close friends even when they stopped dating. But she had never been interested in marriage. So on September 3, 2000, Steinem surprised many when she married South African businessman and environmentalist David Bale, father of actor Christian Bale. The wedding was part civil ceremony and part Cherokee tradition. Charlie Soap, the husband of her good friend Wilma Mankiller, performed the Cherokee portion of the ceremony. Steinem dressed in jeans and a T-shirt. Bale wore black jeans and a black shirt. When asked why she changed her idea about marriage, Steinem reasoned, "I did not change; the idea of marriage did."

At 71 years old, Gloria Steinem has spent half her life in the service of women.

Steinem viewed her marriage to David Bale as a partnership.

Unfortunately, Steinem's marriage was short-lived. On December 30, 2003, Bale died of brain cancer. Steinem continues to speak of him fondly, and she shares her thoughts about grief with others. "He had the greatest heart of anyone I've ever known," Steinem has said. She appreciates that Wilma Mankiller was with her for David's passing, just as she was there as Steinem and Bale began their life together.

After her husband's death, Steinem threw herself into her work. On April 25, 2004, she took part in a historic gathering in Washington, D.C. Steinem and others took part in the March for Women's Lives. They marched to demand political and social justice for women and girls, regardless of age, race, religion, sexual orientation, or economic status. The event kept women's issues in the public view. More than 1 million people came together for the march. It was the largest crowd that had ever gathered in the history of the United States.

On February 8, 2005, Steinem took part in another large gathering—this time as a speaker. An overflow crowd of more than 700 people gathered at Boise State University to hear Gloria Steinem give an address on the state of the women's movement. Men and women of all ages and backgrounds made

Native American activist and leader Wilma Mankiller served as principal chief of the Cherokee Nation from 1985 to 1995. She was the first woman ever to hold that position and, despite early opposition, soon became one of the most respected Cherokee leaders. Mankiller and Steinem met in 1987 when Mankiller was honored as Ms. magazine's Woman of the Year.

up the audience. The crowd listened as the president of the university's Women's Center introduced Steinem as "a woman who has literally changed the course of history."

Steinem banged on the doors that kept her out of places she wanted to go. She tirelessly worked to disprove the belief that women were inferior. She became an inspiring leader. She marched forward and blazed a trail of equality. Steinem, along with many other like-minded feminists, has indeed changed history. And she continues to do so as more and more people recognize women's rights as a worldwide social issue.

In September 2005, Steinem was honored by the Center for the Advancement of Women for her vision and leadership in advancing the rights of and opportunities for women. This honor, as well as many others she has received over the course of her career, was given by an organization that would not have existed without the tireless efforts of Steinem and her fellow feminists. But it is in the increased opportunities, the higher pay, and the hard-won rights now available to all women that Gloria Steinem is truly honored.

Steinem continues to speak and write about women's issues. She is currently at work on *Road to the Heart: America as if Everyone Mattered*, a book about her more than 30 years on the road as a feminist organizer. With *Ms.* as a model, she is part of an effort to form a women's media center and a woman-controlled radio network. She is still a consulting editor at *Ms.*, and the magazine she helped found continues to find readers in many countries. The Prison and Shelter Program also brings *Ms.* to women

In 2004, Ms. magazine honored the activist widows of the September 11 tragedy.

WINTER 2004/2005

WHO'S LOUD, PROUD AND 37 MILLION STRONG?
Answer, page 64

WOMEN OF THE YEAR
The Jersey Girls
THE 9/11 WIDOWS WHO FOUGHT THE BATTLES, SOUGHT THE TRUTH AND WON PLUS:

STRENGTH IN NUMBERS:
Patty Casazza,
Kristen Breitweiser,
Mindy Kleinberg,
and Lorie Van Auken

Kathy Najimy
Maxine Waters
Samantha Power
Saudatu Mahdi
Betty Dukes
Lisa Fernandez

In September 2005, former Secretary of State Madeleine Albright (left), Paramount Pictures CEO Sherry Lansing, and Gloria Steinem were honored as Women Who Changed the Landscape for Women.

behind bars. Jailed women, as well as those living in shelters for abused women, receive free copies of the magazine. The program brings a feminist message to those who need it most.

Women and other oppressed people today receive more support than ever before. Steinem has played a big role in making this a reality. She has spent a lifetime making sure that society no longer holds women back. Girls become astronauts, senators, surgeons, principals, and more in today's world. Steinem says, "Now we know unfairness when we see it, and that's progress." However, she adds, "We've made a good beginning, but it's only a beginning. We haven't even begun to imagine what could be."

Even today, the term feminist is misunderstood by many. According to Steinem, feminism is simply the belief in full social, economic, and political equality of men and women, and "that means both women and men can be and should be feminists." Steinem believes that "in the end, it's not about masculine, feminist, or hyper-feminist; it's about humanity."

STEINEM'S LIFE

1944
Parents divorce;
becomes mother's
caretaker

1934
Born on March 25
in Toledo, Ohio

1951
Moves to
Washington, D.C., to
live with her sister
Susanne; graduates
from Western High
School on June 12

1950

1933
Nazi leader
Adolf Hitler is
named chancellor
of Germany

1945
World War II
(1939-1945) ends

1951
Libya gains its
independence
with help from the
United Nations

WORLD EVENTS

1957

Studies in India; becomes involved with peaceful protests

1969

Covers a Redstockings rally and becomes committed to the women's movement

1956

Graduates from Smith College; has an abortion in England before traveling to India

1960

1962

Pope John XXIII calls the Second Vatican Council, modernizing Roman Catholicism

1959

Fidel Castro becomes leader of Cuba

1969

U.S. astronauts are the first humans to land on the moon

STEINEM'S LIFE

1970

Wins Penney-Missouri Journalism Award for her first feminist piece of writing; begins lecturing around the country on feminist issues

1971

Co-founds the National Women's Political Caucus with other feminist leaders

1972

Helps found *Ms.* magazine; is selected as the spokesperson for the National Women's Political Caucus at the Democratic Presidential Convention

1970

1971

The first microprocessor is produced by Intel

1973

Arab oil embargo creates concerns about natural resources

WORLD EVENTS

1977

Serves on the commission for the National Women's Conference

1983

Publishes *Outrageous Acts and Everyday Rebellions,* a book of essays

1986

Diagnosed with and treated for breast cancer

1985

1976

U.S. military academies admit women

1983

The AIDS (acquired immune deficiency syndrome) virus is identified

1986

The U.S. space shuttle *Challenger* explodes, killing all seven astronauts on board

STEINEM'S LIFE

1992

Publishes
*Revolution from
Within: A Book
of Self-Esteem*

1993

Inducted into
the National
Women's Hall
of Fame

1994

Publishes
*Moving
Beyond
Words*

1995

1991

The Soviet Union
collapses and is replaced
by the Commonwealth of
Independent States

1994

Genocide of
500,000 to
1 million of the
minority Tutsi
group by rival
Hutu people
in Rwanda

WORLD EVENTS

2000

Marries David Bale on September 3; he dies in 2003

2004

Takes part in the March for Women's Lives, the largest gathering in the history of the United States

2005

Honored by the Center for the Advancement of Women for her vision and leadership

2001

Terrorist attacks on the two World Trade Center towers in New York City and on the Pentagon in Washington, D.C., leave thousands dead

2004

Huge tsunami strikes nations bordering the Indian Ocean, killing more than 150,000 people and leaving millions homeless

2005

Major earthquake kills thousands in Pakistan

DATE OF BIRTH: March 25, 1934

BIRTHPLACE: Toledo, Ohio

FATHER: Leo Steinem
(1897–1961)

MOTHER: Ruth Nuneviller Steinem
(1898–1981)

EDUCATION: Smith College

SPOUSE: David Bales
(1941–2003)

DATE OF MARRIAGE: September 3, 2000

Further Reading

Gorman, Jacqueline Laks. *Gloria Steinem: Trailblazers of the Modern World*. Milwaukee: World Almanac Library, 2004.

Hooks, Bell. *Feminism Is for Everybody: Passionate Politics*. Cambridge, Mass.: South End Press, 2000.

Marcello, Patricia Cronin. *Gloria Steinem: A Biography*. Westport, Conn.: Greenwood Press, 2004.

Look for more Signature Lives
books about this era:

Andrew Carnegie: *Captain of Industry*
ISBN 0-7565-0995-5

Carrie Chapman Catt: *A Voice for Women*
ISBN 0-7565-0991-2

Henry B. Gonzalez: *Congressman of the People*
ISBN 0-7565-0996-3

J. Edgar Hoover: *Controversial FBI Director*
ISBN 0-7565-0997-1

Langston Hughes: *The Voice of Harlem*
ISBN 0-7565-0993-9

Douglas MacArthur: *America's General*
ISBN 0-7565-0994-7

Eleanor Roosevelt: *First Lady of the World*
ISBN 0-7565-0992-0

Franklin Roosevelt: *The New Deal President*
ISBN 0-7565-1586-6

Elizabeth Cady Stanton: *Social Reformer*
ISBN 0-7565-0990-4

Wilma Mankiller: *Chief of the Cherokee Nation*
ISBN 0-7565-1600-5

ON THE WEB

For more information on *Gloria Steinem*, use FactHound.

1. Go to *www.facthound.com*
2. Type in a search word related to this book or this book ID: 0756515874
3. Click on the *Fetch It* button.

FactHound will find the best
Web sites for you.

HISTORIC SITES

International Museum of Women
Pier 26
San Francisco, CA 94119
415/543-4669
Permanent and traveling exhibits honor
the accomplishments of women around
the world

The Women's Museum
3800 Parry Ave.
Dallas, TX 75226
214/915-0860
Interactive exhibits honor the past and
explore the contributions of women

abortion
spontaneous or induced termination of
a pregnancy

advocate
person who pleads for or supports a cause

caste
an Indian social class to which a person belongs
by birth

conservative
someone who opposes major change and prefers
things to stay as they are or used to be

discrimination
treating people unfairly because of their race,
religion, sex, or age

feminist
a person who believes in the full social, political,
and economic equality of women

political activist
a person who strives to change a point or idea
in politics

progressive
characterized by progress; moving on or forward

radical
person who favors rapid sweeping changes in
laws or government

Source Notes

Chapter 2

Page 20, line 7: Carolyn G. Heilbrun. *The Education of a Woman: The Life of Gloria Steinem.* New York: The Dial Press, 1995, p. 16.

Page 20, line 17: Gloria Steinem. E-mail interview. 24 Feb. 2005.

Page 22, line 1: Gloria Steinem. *Revolution from Within.* Boston: Little Brown, 1992, p. 65.

Page 23, line 4: *The Education of a Woman: The Life of Gloria Steinem,* pp. 20–21.

Chapter 3

Page 26, line 20: Gloria Steinem. E-mail interview. 24 Feb. 2005.

Page 29, line 1: Gloria Steinem. *Outrageous Acts and Everyday Rebellions.* New York: Henry Holt, 1983, p. 30.

Page 30, line 1: Ibid., p. 145.

Page 31, line 10: *The Education of a Woman: The Life of Gloria Steinem,* p. 27.

Page 31, line 24: Ibid., p. 31.

Chapter 4

Page 43, line 18: Gloria Steinem. *Moving Beyond Words.* New York: Simon & Schuster, 1994, p. 266.

Page 43, line 25: Ibid., pp. 266–267.

Chapter 5

Page 48, line 14: *Outrageous Acts and Everyday Rebellions,* pp. 15–16.

Page 49, line 6: Ibid., p. 21.

Page 51, line 3: Ibid., p. 89.

Chapter 6

Page 57, line 18: Ibid., p. 21.

Page 58, line 7: Ibid.

Page 58, line 14: Ibid.

Page 60, line 9: *The Education of a Woman: The Life of Gloria Steinem,* p. 204.

Page 60, line 20: *Outrageous Acts and Everyday Rebellions,* p. 30.

Page 60, line 27: Equal Rights Amendment. 5 Dec. 2005. www.equal-rightsamendment.org/overview.htm

Page 62, line 1: Gloria Steinem. "Testimony Before Senate Hearings on Equal Rights Amendment." 6 May 1970. 28 Jan. 2005. www.history.org/sources/steinem.html

Page 62, line 8: Ibid.

Page 64, line 2: *Outrageous Acts and Everyday Rebellions*, p. 151.

Chapter 7

Page 67, line 8: *The Education of a Woman: The Life of Gloria Steinem*, p. 196.

Page 68, line 4: Ibid., p. 197.

Page 70, sidebar: Ibid., p. 231.

Page 74, line 8: *Revolution from Within*, p. 157.

Chapter 8

Page 80, line 9: *The Education of a Woman: The Life of Gloria Steinem*, p. 316.

Page 81, line 13: *Revolution from Within*, p. 55.

Page 83, line 21: *Outrageous Acts and Everyday Rebellions*, p. 158.

Page 84, line 3: *Revolution from Within*, p. 245.

Page 84, line 5: Ibid.

Page 86, line 12: *Moving Beyond Words*, p. 283.

Page 86, line 20: Gloria Steinem. E-mail interview. 15 March 2005.

Chapter 9

Page 89, line 14: Gloria Steinem. Lecture, Boise State University, 8 Feb. 2005.

Page 91, line 2: "David Bale, Husband of Gloria Steinem, Dies at 62." *CNN.com*. 1 Jan. 2004. 5 Dec. 2005. www.cnn.com

Page 92, line 3: President of Boise State's Women's Center. "Introduction of Gloria Steinem." Lecture, Boise State University, 8 Feb. 2005.

Page 95, sidebar: Mariana Bekker. "She Walks, She Talks, She's a Feminist ... Gloria Steinem Speaks at Boise State." *Arbiter Online*. 10 Feb. 2005. 5 Dec. 2005. www.arbiteronline.com/vnews/display.v/ART/2005/02/10/420adfd4cea24

Page 95, line 11: Gloria Steinem. E-mail interview. 15 March 2005.

Page 95, line 13: Christina Frank. "Life as a Lightning Rod: Gloria Steinem on Feminism, Aging, and Why She Got Married." *Biography*. March 2002, p. 104.

Banner, Lois W. *Women in Modern America: A Brief History*. Fort Worth, Texas: Harcourt Brace College Publishers, 1995.

"Gloria Steinem." *Newsweek*. August 16, 1971, pp. 51–55.

Heilbrun, Carolyn G. *The Education of a Woman: The Life of Gloria Steinem*. New York: The Dial Press, 1995.

Langway, Lynn, Nancy Cooper, Lucy Howard, and Gloria Borger. "Steinem at 50: Gloria in Excelsis." *Newsweek*. June 4, 1984, p. 27.

Lorber, Judith. *Gender Inequality: Feminist Theories and Politics*. Los Angeles: Roxbury Publishing Company, 1998.

Martin, Jane Roland. *Coming of Age in Academe: Rekindling Women's Hopes and Reforming the Academy*. New York: Routledge, 2000.

Steinem, Gloria. *Outrageous Acts and Everyday Rebellions*. New York: Henry Holt, 1983.

Steinem, Gloria. *Revolution from Within: A Book of Self-Esteem*. Boston: Little, Brown and Company, 1992.

Steinem, Gloria. *Moving Beyond Words*. New York: Simon & Schuster, 1994.

Steinem, Gloria. "Sex, Lies, and Advertising." In *Women: A Feminist Perspective*. Jo Freeman, ed. Mountain View, Calif.: Mayfield Publishing, 1995.

Steinem, Gloria. "Men and Women Talking." In *Counterbalance: Gendered Perspectives for Writing and Language*. Carolyn Logan, ed. Peterborough, Ontario: Broadview Press, 1997.

Steinem, Gloria. "Advice to Old Fems." *Ms*. February/March 2000, pp. 93–95.

Watkins, Bonnie, and Nina Rothschild. *In the Company of Women: Voices from the Women's Movement*. St. Paul, Minn.: Minnesota Historical Press, 1996.

Nancy Garhan Attebury is the author of many magazine pieces for children and several non-fiction books for educational publishers. She has a master's degree in children's literature from Hollins University in Virginia. Nancy lives in LaGrande, Oregon, with her husband, Rich. Their children, Ramirose and Garhan, are grown.

Image Credits